W9-CLC-464

8604 9100 035 809 0

Sing-Along Holiday Stories

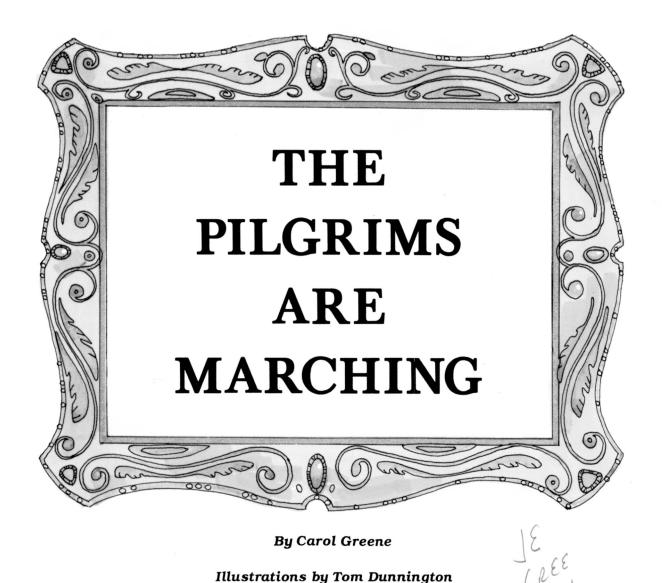

THE PILGRIMS ARE MARCHING

By Carol Greene

Illustrations by Tom Dunnington

JE
GREE
c.1

CHILDRENS PRESS ®

CHICAGO

This book is for Daniel Ruhlin.

Library of Congress Cataloging-in-Publication Data

Greene, Carol.
  The pilgrims are marching / by Carol Greene.
    p.   cm. — (A Sing-Along Holiday Story)
  Summary: The adventurous Johnny B. and the other Pilgrims sail to
America and prepare for the first Thanksgiving, as described in
counting verses from one to ten.
  ISBN 0-516-08234-5
  1. Folk songs, English—United States. [1. Pilgrims (New
Plymouth Colony)—Songs and music.   2.   Thanksgiving Day—Songs and
music.   3.   Folk songs, American.   4.   Counting.] I. Title.
II. Series.
PZ8.3.G82Pi   1989   88-20219
                                                CIP
                                                AC

Childrens Press®, Chicago
Copyright © 1988 by Regensteiner Publishing Enterprises, Inc.
All rights reserved. Published simultaneously in Canada.
Printed in the United States of America.
    3 4 5 6 7 8 9 10 R 97 96 95 94 93 92

Here come the Pilgrims!

65.96 UBS 15.98

The Pilgrims are marching one by one.
Away! Away!
The Pilgrims are marching one by one.
Away! Away!
Into the *Mayflower*, over the sea,
And one of the children is young Johnny B.,
As they all go marching off
to the land
of the brave
and the free.

The Pilgrims are landing two by two.
Hurrah! Hurrah!
The Pilgrims are landing two by two.
Hurrah! Hurrah!
Ninety-nine people, a dog and a pup,
And young Johnny B. almost blows them all up,
As they all step proudly down
to the land
of the brave
and the free.

The Pilgrims are building three by three.
Thump thump! Thump thump!
The Pilgrims are building three by three.
Thump thump! Thump thump!
House after house in a neat little row,
And young Johnny B. somehow hammers his toe,
As they all work long and hard
in the land
of the brave
and the free.

The Pilgrims are shivering four by four.
Oh dear! Oh dear!
The Pilgrims are shivering four by four.
Oh dear! Oh dear!
Snow piles up high in a fierce winter storm,
And young Johnny B. jumps to keep himself warm,
As they shake and shiver there
in the land
of the brave
and the free.

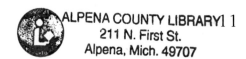
ALPENA COUNTY LIBRARY 1 1
211 N. First St.
Alpena, Mich. 49707

The Pilgrims are visiting five by five.
Come in! Come in!
The Pilgrims are visiting five by five.
Come in! Come in!
Indian neighbors bring much good advice,
And young Johnny B. tries to give them his mice,
As they sit and visit there
in the land
of the brave
and the free.

13

The Pilgrims are planting six by six.
Dig deep! Dig deep!
The Pilgrims are planting six by six.
Dig deep! Dig deep!
Indian corn in one row, then another,
And young Johnny B. almost buries his brother,
As they plant their first spring crop
in the land
of the brave
and the free.

The Pilgrims are searching seven by seven.
Look here! Look there!
The Pilgrims are searching seven by seven.
Look here! Look there!
Searching for Johnny who's got himself lost,
They promise they'll find him whatever the cost,
As they wander here and there
in the land
of the brave
and the free.

The Pilgrims are rowing eight by eight.
Heave ho! Heave ho!
The Pilgrims are rowing eight by eight.
Heave ho! Heave ho!
Looking for Johnny, their boat runs aground.
The Indians have him! He's safe and he's sound,
As they all go rowing home
in the land
of the brave
and the free.

The Pilgrims are harvesting nine by nine.
Chop chop! Chop chop!
The Pilgrims are harvesting nine by nine.
Chop chop! Chop chop!
Up and then down all the fine golden rows,
And young Johnny B. gets a sting on the nose,
As they gather in their crops
in the land
of the brave
and the free.

The Pilgrims are cooking ten by ten.
Sniff sniff! Sniff sniff!
The Pilgrims are cooking ten by ten.
Sniff sniff! Sniff sniff!
Stirring and mixing and making a lot,
And young Johnny B. almost falls in a pot,
As they cook their first big feast
in the land
of the brave
and the free.

The Pilgrims and Indians feast together.
Yum yum! Yum yum!
The Pilgrims and Indians feast together.
Yum yum! Yum yum!
Turkeys and lobsters and biscuits and cake,
And young Johnny B. gets the worst stomach ache,
As they all sit down and feast
in the land
of the brave
and the free.

The Pilgrims and Indians all give thanks.
Amen! Amen!
The Pilgrims and Indians all give thanks.
Amen! Amen!
Heads bowed, they offer their prayers gratefully.
They even feel thankful for young Johnny B.,
As they all give thanks to God
for the land
of the brave
and the free.

THE PILGRIMS ARE MARCHING

Carol Greene

Irish and American Folksong

The Pilgrims are marching one by one. A-way!   A-way!   The

Pilgrims are marching one by one. Away!   Away!   Into the Mayflower,

o·ver the sea, and one of the children is young Johnny B., As they all go

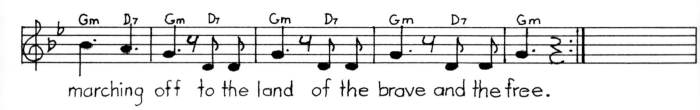

marching off to the land of the brave and the free.

2. The Pilgrims are landing two by two. Hur·rah! Hur·rah!
The Pilgrims are landing two by two. Hur·rah! Hur·rah!
Nine·ty·nine peo·ple, a dog and a pup,
And young John·ny B. almost blows them all up,
As they all step proudly down to the land
of the brave and the free.

3. The Pilgrims are building three by three. Thump,Thump! Thump,Thump!
The Pilgrims are building three by three. Thump,Thump! Thump,Thump!
House after house in a neat little row,
And young John·ny B. some·how ham·mers his toe,
As they all work long and hard in the land
of the brave and the free.

4. The Pilgrims are shiv·er·ing four by four. Oh dear! Oh dear!
The Pilgrims are shiv·er·ing four by four. Oh dear! Oh dear!
Snow piles up high in a fierce winter storm,
And young John·ny B. jumps to keep himself warm,
As they shake and shiv·er there in the land
of the brave and the free.

5. The Pilgrims are visiting five by five. Come in! Come in!
The Pilgrims are visiting five by five. Come in! Come in!
In·di·an neigh·bors bring much good advice,
And young John·ny B. tries to give them his mice,
As they sit and vi·sit there in the land
of the brave and the free.

6. The Pilgrims are planting six by six. Dig deep! Dig deep!
The Pilgrims are planting six by six. Dig deep! Dig deep!
Indian corn in one row then an·oth·er,
And young John·ny B. al·most buries his brother,
As they plant their first spring crop in the land
of the brave and the free.

29

7. The Pilgrims are searching seven by seven. Look here! Look there!
The Pilgrims are searching seven by seven. Look here! Look there
Searching for Johnny who got himself lost,
They promise they'll find him whatever the cost,
As they wander here and there in the land
of the brave and the free.

8. The Pilgrims are rowing eight by eight. Heave ho! Heave ho!
The Pilgrims are rowing eight by eight. Heave ho! Heave ho!
Looking for Johnny, their boat runs aground.
The Indians have him! He's safe and he's sound,
As they all go rowing home in the land
of the brave and the free.

9. The Pilgrims are harvesting nine by nine. Chop chop! Chop chop!
The Pilgrims are harvesting nine by nine. Chop chop! Chop chop!
Up and then down all the fine golden rows,
And young Johnny B. gets a sting on the nose,
As they gather in their crops in the land
of the brave and the free.

10. The Pilgrims are cooking ten by ten. Sniff sniff! Sniff sniff!
The Pilgrims are cooking ten by ten. Sniff sniff! Sniff sniff!
Stirring and mixing and making a lot,
And young Johnny B. almost falls in the pot,
As they cook their first big feast in the land
of the brave and the free.

11. The Pilgrims and Indians feast together. Yum yum! Yum yum!
The Pilgrims and Indians feast together. Yum yum! Yum yum!
Turkeys and lobsters and biscuits and cake,
And young Johnny B. gets the worst stomach ache,
As they all sit down and feast in the land
of the brave and the free.

12. The Pilgrims and Indians all give thanks. Amen! Amen!
The Pilgrims and Indians all give thanks. Amen! Amen!
Heads bowed, they offered their prayers gratefully,
They even feel thankful for young Johnny B.,
As they all give thanks to God for the land
of the brave and the free.

NOTE

About thirty children came across the ocean on the *Mayflower*. One of them was a boy called John Billington. He was a lively boy, just like Johnny B. in the song. He probably didn't do *all* the things Johnny B. did. But he did *some* of them.

The *Mayflower* first landed at a place called Provincetown, on the coast of Cape Cod. While the ship was there, John Billington opened a keg of gunpowder and almost blew everyone up.

The next July, he got himself lost in the woods. For five days he ate berries and whatever else he could find. Then a tribe of Indians found *him*. They took care of John until some Pilgrims in a boat came to take him home.

John had a brother called Francis. He was lively too. One day he went exploring. He came home and told everyone he had found the Pacific Ocean. Actually, all he'd found was a big pond. But the rest of the Pilgrims named it Billington's Sea in honor of him anyway.

Many pictures show the Pilgrims in black clothes. But the records they kept show that they wore bright clothes most of the time. John and Francis' clothes might have been red, green, purple, or bright blue.

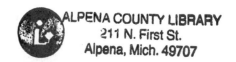
ALPENA COUNTY LIBRARY
211 N. First St.
Alpena, Mich. 49707

About the Author

Carol Greene has a B.A. in English Literature from Park College, Parkville, Missouri, and an M.A. in Musicology from Indiana University, Bloomington. She's worked with international exchange programs, taught music and writing, and edited children's books. She now works as a free-lance writer in St. Louis, Missouri and has had published over 20 books for children and a few for adults. When she isn't writing, Ms. Greene likes to read, travel, sing, and do volunteer work at her church. Her other books for Childrens Press include: *The Super Snoops and the Missing Sleepers; Sandra Day O'Connor: First Woman on the Supreme Court; Rain! Rain!; Please, Wind?; Snow Joe;* and *The New True Book of Holidays Around the World.*

About the Artist

Tom Dunnington divides his time between book illustration and wildlife painting. He has done many books for Childrens Press, as well as working on textbooks, and is a regular contributor to *Highlights for Children.* Tom lives in Oak Park, Illinois.